MASTERING NON-VERBAL REASONING

MASTERING
NON-VERBAL
REASONING

THE SECRETS TO PASSING
NON-VERBAL REASONING EXAMS, EXPOSED

Terrence Millington

DISCLAIMER
This book contains information and techniques which have been used by the author for several years. The information detailed in
this book is to the author's best knowledge and experiences, and there are no claims for their guaranteed effectiveness. They are to
be used by the reader at their own liability. It may or may not be beneficial depending on one's stage of development. The use of
the material offered in this book is totally at the reader's own responsibility and the author of this book is not responsible or liable
in any manner whatsoever.

Matador
9 Priory Business Park
Kibworth Beauchamp
Leicestershire LE8 0RX, UK
Tel: (+44) 116 279 2299
Fax: (+44) 116 279 2277
Email: books@troubador.co.uk
Web: www.troubador.co.uk/matador

ISBN 978-1783064-571

British Library Cataloguing in Publication Data.
A catalogue record for this book is available from the British Library.

Typeset in Aldine by Troubador Publishing Ltd

Matador is an imprint of Troubador Publishing Ltd
Printed and bound by CPI Group (UK) Ltd, Croydon, CR0 4YY

ACKNOWLEDGEMENTS

I would like to thank my grandmother for teaching me the concepts of non-verbal reasoning and giving me the opportunity to attend an independent school.

My father, Wayne for his continued support and faith in me over the years and also for motivating me to actually write this book and not just keep promising to do so.

My friend, Cory who helped to illustrate the book by digitizing my hand – drawn images and questions.

To Patsy and my godfather, Andre for proof reading (the book) and offering constructive feedback within the given deadline.

All of the children I have taught over the years, for the memories and fun times that made teaching the subject enjoyable.

And last but far from least, my fiancée Cigdem for her continuous support and encouragement.

This book is dedicated to my brothers and sisters.

PREFACE

This book is the culmination of having passed an 11+ entrance examination to an independent school and more than ten years of teaching and preparing children for entrance examinations to various independent and grammar schools.

My love for non-verbal reasoning started when I was ten years old practising for the 11+ examination. Most areas of the subject seemed so simple to me. Perhaps I was one of the lucky ones you could say! Almost seven years later I began teaching both verbal and non-verbal reasoning. I found that I enjoyed the challenge of passing on this knowledge to my students and enabling them to pass the tests, scoring high marks.

Due to many years of teaching, I came up with my 'Secret Notes' that I shared with the children I taught. These formed a series of steps, hints and tips for working out non-verbal questions. I like to refer to these notes as 'fail proof!' especially as a high percentage of children that I taught (in a group setting) passed the examination. These 'secret notes' have been perfected over the years and I have now reproduced them in a format that emulates my teaching style.

My goal is to help children to understand the concept of non-verbal reasoning so that they achieve the highest marks possible when doing a non-verbal paper. I hope this book will also help parents to understand the subject so they can help their children.

Thank you for purchasing this book. Please read the 'Message to Parents' section for advice on how to get the best out of this book.

MESSAGE TO PARENTS

Although this book is mainly geared towards children practising for 11+ entrance exams, it is also a guide for parents who would like to help their children with non-verbal reasoning but who have little or no understanding of the subject. I have made it easy for parents to familiarise themselves with the types of questions that may come up and the techniques for solving them.

In order to get the best usage out of this book, I suggest that at least once a fortnight you quiz your child on the methods and techniques laid out in the book. I cannot stress enough how important learning the methods and techniques are. I tend to liken it to mathematical formulae: if you understand the method behind the formula to a question and remember it, you can solve any question that is similar. In my experience this is also the case for non-verbal reasoning.

A minimum of three and a half hours a week should be put into learning and practising non-verbal for the best results. There are obvious exceptions to that. If your child is weak (scoring lower than 75% in tests) then they should be practicing more. If your child is very strong (scoring over 90% consistently in tests) then the time spent practising may be lowered. However I would not recommend less than two hours a week minimum practice time, even with the smartest child, as complacency and forgetfulness can easily set in.

HOW TO USE THIS BOOK

Learn the methods and techniques for each topic and ask a parent or friend to test you on the 'Steps' or 'Things to Look For' at least once every two weeks.

Make sure you follow the procedures for working out each topic as they are laid out in this book. Do not try and rush the process.

Once you have mastered the methods and techniques (i.e. you have learnt and can remember all of the 'Steps' and 'Things to Look For' in each topic), you can then start to use little shortcuts you may have found.

Remember that this book will help you to answer any question in the topics covered. If you are stuck on any question from one of these topics on any other paper then use this book to help you work it out.

Remember that it is better to learn the way to answer questions than to just learn the answer. So please learn these methods and techniques if you want to attain the highest possible scores in any non-verbal reasoning test.

Write wherever you like on the book, this is YOUR notebook now, so draw, write down or highlight anything that will help you to answer the questions, or remember things when practising or revising in the future.

THIS NOTEBOOK BELONGS TO

_____

When you feel like you have mastered a topic, cross it off the list below so that you know which topics you need to concentrate more on.

ANALOGIES

CODES

ODD ONE OUT

SEQUENCES

MOST IN COMMON

MATRICES

ANALOGIES

Step 1:
Break down the first picture they give you. (The question analogy.)

Step 2:
Take one thing out of the broken down picture and view the transformation. (See how it changes.)

Step 3:
Now go to the answer picture and emulate what you did from step 2. (Copy the change from Step 2 using the appropriate shape in the answer picture.)

★★You can now eliminate incorrect answers★★

Step 4:
Go back to Step 2 and repeat as necessary.

THINGS TO LOOK FOR

(This will help you with Step 2.)

- Rotation/direction
- Size change (small, big, medium etc.)
- Shaded/un-shaded
- Horizontal/vertical lines
- Outline of shape (dotted, thin, thick, solid etc.)
- Number of shapes/symbols
- Replacement (when one shape/symbol takes the place of another shape/symbol)
- Patterns (curvy, straight, dotted etc.)
- Grouping (shapes/symbols joining together)
- Shape change
- Overlapping/under-lapping
- Reflection/mirroring
- What things stay the same?

1

Analogies Questions

1

A B C D E

2

A B C D E

3

A B C D E

4

A B C D E

5

A B C D E

First try to answer these using the notes

1) ____   2) ____   3) ____   4) ____   5) ____

Working out ANALOGIES

Q1)

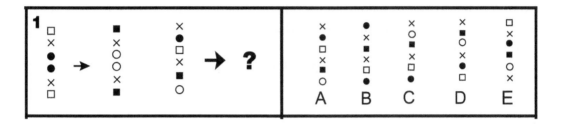

Step 1:

☐
✕
●
●
✕
☐

When breaking down the first picture you should have found the following:
a) There are two crosses
b) There are two un-shaded squares
c) There are two shaded circles

Step 2:
Take one of the things you found and view the transformation. (I'll take 'b'.)

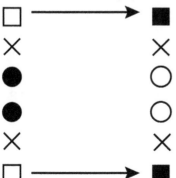

b) There are two unshaded squares – you should see that the unshaded squares stay in the same position but become shaded.

Step 3:
Now go to the answer question and use what you have just found to filter out wrong answers. You are looking for the answers where the squares are in the same place as the question, but have the opposite shade.
You should have eliminated answers 'D' and 'E'.

Step 4:
Now go back and take another thing you found in Step 1 and view the transformation. (I'll take 'a'.)

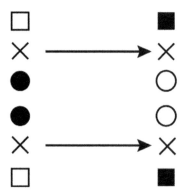

a) There are two crosses – you should see that the crosses remain in the same place, nothing else changes about them.

Step 5:
Now go to the answer question and use what you have found to filter out more wrong answers. You were left with answers 'A', 'B' and 'C' from before, and out of those answers, look for the ones that have the crosses in the same position as the question, unchanged.
You should have eliminated 'B'.

Step 6:
Now go back and take another thing you found in Step 1 and view the transformation. You must take 'c'.

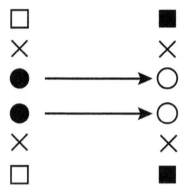

c) There are two shaded circles – you should see that the shaded circles stay in the same position but become un-shaded.

Step 7:
Now go to the answer question and use what you have found to filter out more wrong answers. You were left with answers 'A' and 'C' from before, now you should have eliminated 'A' as although the circles are in the same position, they do not have the opposite shade to the ones in the question.
So the answer is 'C'.

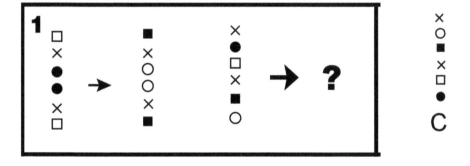

Q2)

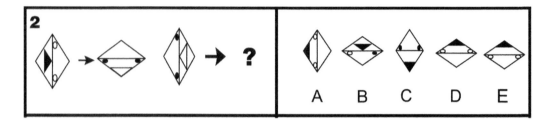

A B C D E

Step 1:

When breaking down the first picture you should have found the following:
a) The main shape is a vertical diamond
b) There is a shaded triangle with the tip perpendicular (at 90°) to the line running down the middle of the diamond
c) There are two un-shaded circles on the same side of the middle line

Step 2:
Take one of the things you found and view the transformation. (I'll take 'a'.)

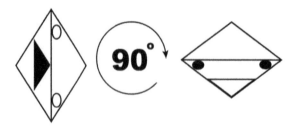

a) The main shape is a vertical diamond – you should see that the diamond rotates 90° clockwise so that it is horizontal.

Step 3:

Now go to the answer question and use what you have just found to filter out wrong answers. You should have eliminated answers 'A' and 'C' as they are the only answer pictures where the diamond is still vertical.

Step 4:

Now go back and take another thing you found in Step 1 and view the transformation. (I'll take 'b'.)

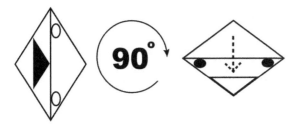

b) There is a shaded triangle with the tip perpendicular to the line running down the middle of the diamond – you should see that the triangle rotates 90° with the diamond. It then fits into the corner on the opposite side of the middle line, and becomes un-shaded.

Step 5:

Now go to the answer question and use what you have found to filter out more wrong answers. Remember, the triangle rotates then fits into the corner on the opposite side of the middle line. You were left with answers 'B', 'D' and 'E' from before so look at only those answers. You should have eliminated 'B' as the triangle is not in the top corner.

Step 6:

Now go back and take another thing you found in Step 1 and view the transformation. You must take 'c'.

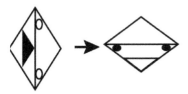

c) There are two un-shaded circles on the same side of the middle line – you should see that the un-shaded circles also rotate with the shape but remain in the same place. They also become shaded.

Step 7:
Now go to the answer question and use what you have found to filter out more wrong answers. You were left with answers 'D' and 'E' from before, now you should have eliminated 'E' because the circles are on the opposite side of the line to where they should be.
So the answer is 'D'.

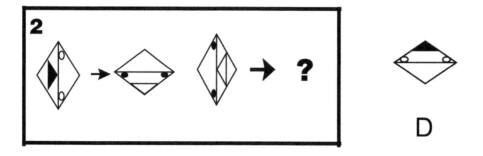

D

Q3)

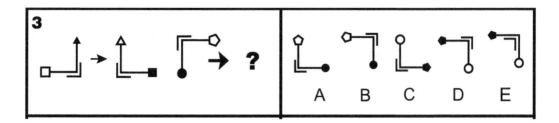

Step 1:

When breaking down the first picture you should have found the following:
a)   There is a right-angled line with a double line on the outside of the right angle
b)   There is a shaded triangle at the top of the line
c)   There is an un-shaded square on the left of the line

Step 2:
Take one of the things you found and view the transformation. (I'll take 'a'.)

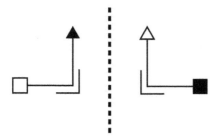

a) There is a right-angled line with a double line on the outside of the right angle – you should see that the line rotates 90° clockwise, or it is a vertical reflection of itself.

Step 3:
Now go to the answer question and use what you have just found to filter out wrong answers. It is easier to use the rotation method here. If it helps, rotate the page to see how the answer picture's line should look. You should have eliminated answers 'A', 'C' and 'E'. Note that 'E' has the double line on the inside of the right angle.

Step 4:
Now go back and take another thing you found in Step 1 and view the transformation. (I'll take 'c'.)

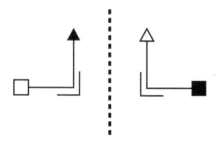

c) There is an un-shaded square on the left of the line – here it is easier to use the reflection method, as when you reflect the shape vertically the square stays in the same position on the line, it just looks like it 'flipped' sides.

Step 5:
Now go to the answer question and use what you have found to filter out more wrong answers. As the pentagon is un-shaded like the square in the first question picture, you will take what you have found from Step 4 using the pentagon. You were left with answers 'B' and 'D' from before, now you should have eliminated 'B' as the pentagon is still un-shaded when it should be shaded. So the answer is 'D'.

Step 6:

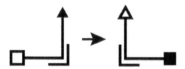

As you already have your answer, this is just to check your work and make sure you are correct. So go back and take another thing you found in Step 1 and view the transformation. You must take 'b'.

b) There is a shaded triangle at the top of the line – you should use the reflection method again here and note that the triangle stays in the same position but becomes un-shaded.

Step 7:
Now go to the answer question and use what you have found to check your answer. As the circle is the shaded shape in the answer question you will use what you have just found on this shape. You should note that the circle stays in the same position and changes to un-shaded like it should. You now know for definite that 'D' is the answer.

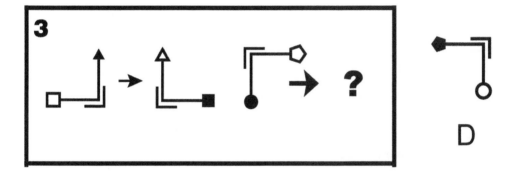

Q4)

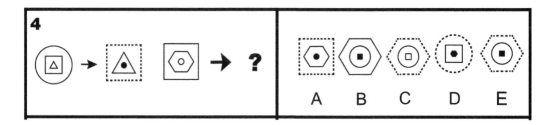

Step 1:

When breaking down the first picture you should have found the following:
a) The largest shape is a circle
b) The medium shape is a square
c) The smallest shape is a triangle

Step 2:
Take one of the things that you have just found and view the transformation. (I'll take 'a'.)

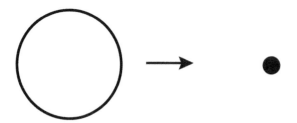

a) The largest shape is a circle – you should see that the circle which is the largest shape, now becomes the smallest and it is shaded.

Step 3:
Now go to the answer question and use what you have just found to filter out wrong answers. In the answer question the largest shape is the square, so you will use what you have found on that. You should have eliminated 'A', 'C' and 'D' as they do not have shaded squares as the smallest shape.

Step 4:
Now go back and take another thing you found in Step 1 and view the transformation. (I'll take 'b'.)

b) The medium shape is a square – you should see that the medium shape which is the square now becomes the biggest shape and the outline is dotted.

Step 5:
Now go to the answer question and use what you have found to filter out more wrong answers. You were left with answers 'B' and 'E' from before, you should now have eliminated 'B' as the outline is not dotted. So the answer is 'E'.

Step 6:
As you already have your answer, this is just to check your work and make sure you are correct. So go back and take another thing you found in Step 1 and view the transformation. You must take 'c'.

c) The smallest shape is a triangle – you should see that the smallest shape which is the triangle, becomes the medium shape.

Step 7:

Now go to the answer question and use what you have found to check your answer. You should see that the circle, which was the smallest shape, is now the medium sized shape, so you know that answer 'E' is correct.

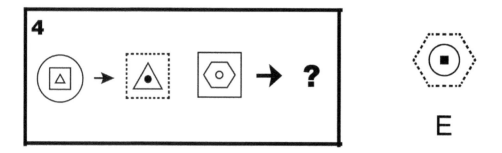

Q5)

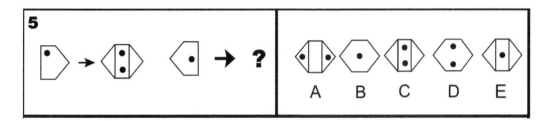

Step 1:

When breaking down the first picture you should have found the following:
a) It is an irregular pentagon with a shaded circle at the top of the straight edged side

Step 2:
As there is only one thing to find, you must choose 'a' and view the transformation.

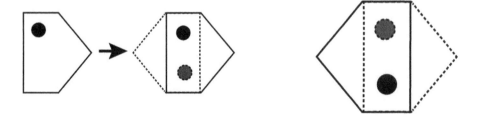

a) It is an irregular pentagon with a shaded circle at the top of the straight edged side –
you should note that the transformation involves placing a replica (exact copy) of the
same shape over the original shape then turning it 180°.

Step 3:
Now go to the answer question and use what you have just found to filter out wrong

answers. The main shape outline in the answer picture you are looking for should look like the shape in the second question picture, so that eliminates answers 'B' and 'D'. Next you have to work out where the shaded circle should be and how many. As the circle is in the middle, when the replica shape overlaps and rotates the circles will end up eclipsing (overlapping) each other, making it look like there is still only one circle in the transformed shape.

Now you should have eliminated answers 'A' and 'C'. So the answer is 'E'.

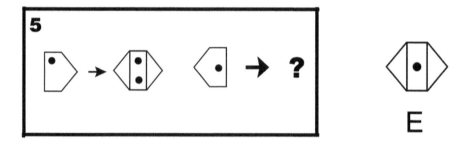

YOUR OWN ADDITIONAL NOTES

Use this page to write down important points you have picked up from this topic, and any additional information you would like to add:

CODES

Step 1:
Don't look at the pictures (cover them with your hand) and find the recurring letters.

Step 2:
Choose one of the recurring letters and find out why they recur. (To do this, you first look at the pictures that contain those letters – find what is the SAME about them, and then check the remaining picture(s) to make sure that what you have found is DIFFERENT from those.)

HINT

If what you have found is the same in any of the
other pictures with a different letter then that is
NOT what you are looking for, try again.

Step 3:
Using what we have found from Step 2 (or Step 4), we go to the answer picture and fill in the part of the answer that you have found.

★★You can now eliminate incorrect answers★★

Step 4:
Take another set of recurring letters and find out why they match. (Using the same method from Step 2.)

Step 5:
Go back to Step 3 and repeat until all of the sets of recurring letters are gone.

IMPORTANT

When there are no more recurring letters left, but there is still an answer to find, this means that the picture you are comparing must always be different but in the same way.

E.g. – All different sizes, all different directions, all different shading, all different shapes etc.

Codes Questions

1

XC	YB	ZD	XE	?

XB	YD	YE	ZE	YC
A	B	C	D	E

2

RQ	SP	TQ	SN	RN	?

SN	RN	TP	SQ	RP
A	B	C	D	E

3

ES	FP	GT	FQ	?

ET	GP	FT	EP	FS
A	B	C	D	E

4

MRT	NRW	PST	?

NRT	PSW	NST	MST	NSW
A	B	C	D	E

5

JPB	KQB	JRC	?

KRC	JQC	JQB	KQC	JRB
A	B	C	D	E

First try to answer these using the notes

1) ____   2) ____   3) ____   4) ____   5) ____

Working out CODES

Q1)

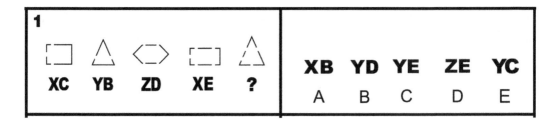

Step 1:
Cover the pictures and find the recurring letters. You should have found the letter 'X'.

Step 2:
As there is only one set of recurring letters, you must choose 'X'. Look at the pictures represented by the letter 'X', and find what is the same.

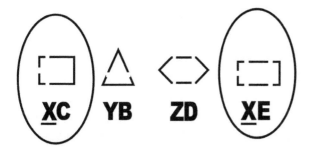

You should have found that the two pictures with the letter 'X' are both the same shape. To make sure that the letter represents the shape, you must now look at the other pictures that aren't represented by an 'X'. The other pictures are different shapes, so you know that the first letter represents the SHAPE. Now you know that 'X' means a rectangle. This also tells you that 'Y' means a triangle and 'Z' means a hexagon.

Step 3:
Now that you know the first letter represents the shape, go to the answer pictures and

filter out the wrong answers. The answer picture is a triangle, so you know that the first letter will be a 'Y'. This eliminates answers 'A' and 'D'.

Step 4:
For this step you are meant to take recurring letters left, but there are no more left. Like the 'IMPORTANT' section in the notes states, this just means that all of the other pictures are different in the same way.

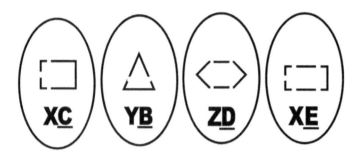

So look at all of the pictures – you should see that all of the pictures are divided into different amounts. So they are the same in that they are all divided, however they are different because the divisions are all different amounts. You now know that the second letter represents the amount that the shape is divided into. 'C' means three parts, 'B' means two parts, 'D' means four parts and 'E' means five parts.

Step 5:
Now that you know what the second letter means, go to the answer picture and eliminate the remaining wrong answers. The answer picture is divided into five segments, so the second letter will be an 'E'.

From earlier you were left with answers 'B', 'C' and 'E'. Now you can fill in the second letter and get your answer. The answer letters are 'YE' so the answer is 'C'.

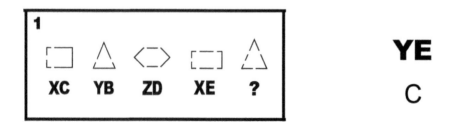

Q2)

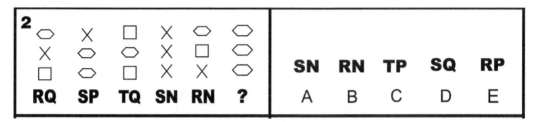

SN	RN	TP	SQ	RP
A	B	C	D	E

Step 1:
Cover the pictures and find the recurring letters. You should have found the letters 'R', 'S', 'N' and 'Q'.

Step 2:
It doesn't matter which recurring letters you choose to work out first. (I am going to pick 'N' to work out first.) So look at the pictures represented by the letter 'N' and find what is the same in them.

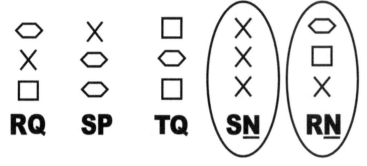

You should have found that both of the pictures have a cross as the bottom shape. To make sure that the last letter represents that shape, now look at the other pictures. You should spot that two other pictures end in the same shapes, so check the last letters to those pictures, they are the same so you now know that the last letter definitely represents the bottom shape in the picture. You have found that 'N' means a cross, 'Q' means a square and 'P' means a hexagon at the bottom of the picture.

Step 3:
Now that you know the first letter represents the bottom shape in the picture, go to the answer pictures and filter out the wrong answers. The bottom shape in the answer picture is a hexagon, so the last letter will be a 'P'. This eliminates answers 'A', 'B' and 'D'.

Step 4:
Now take another set of recurring letters, not 'Q' as you have already worked this out during Step 2. I'll pick 'R' to work out. Look at the pictures containing the letter 'R' and find what is the same in them.

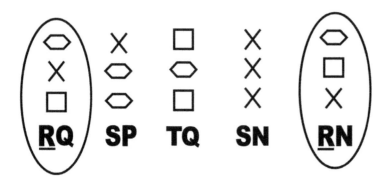

You should have found that both pictures have a hexagon as the top shape, you will also see that both contain a square. So now you have to check the other pictures to find out which of those two possibilities it is. There are other pictures that have a square, so this cannot be what the 'R' stands for, however no other pictures have a hexagon as the top shape, so this must be what 'R' means.

Now you know that the first letter represents the top shape of the picture. 'R' means a hexagon, 'S' means a cross and 'T' means a square.

Step 5:
Now that you know what the first letter means, go to the answer picture and eliminate the remaining wrong answer. The answer picture has a hexagon as the top shape, so the first letter will be an 'R'.

From earlier you were left with answers 'C' and 'E'. Now you can fill in the first letter and get your answer. The answer letters are 'RP' so the answer is 'E'.

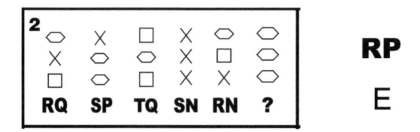

Q3)

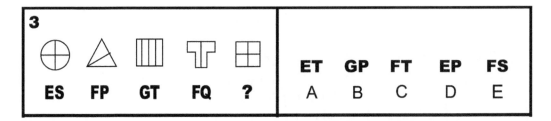

					ET	GP	FT	EP	FS
					A	B	C	D	E

Step 1:

Cover the pictures and find the recurring letters. You should have found the letter 'F'.

Step 2:

As there is only one set of recurring letters, you must choose 'F'. Look at the pictures represented by the letter 'F' and find what is the same.

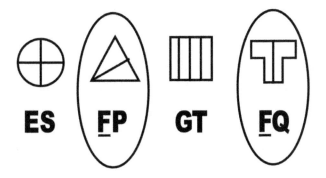

You should have found that the two pictures with the letter 'F' are both divided in half. To make sure that the letter represents the division you must now look at the other pictures that aren't represented by an 'F'. The other pictures are divided into different amounts, so you know that the first letter represents the amount of segments the picture has. 'F' means divided in half, 'E' means divided into four and 'G' means divided into five.

Step 3:

Now that you know the first letter represents the amount of segments the picture is divided into, go to the answer pictures and filter out the wrong answers. The answer picture is divided into four segments, so you know the first letter will be an 'E'. This eliminates answers 'B', 'C' and 'E'.

Step 4:

For this step you are meant to take another set of recurring letters, but there are no more left. This just means that all of the other pictures are different in the same way.

So look at all of the pictures, you should see that all of the pictures are shapes, and they are all different. So the last letter must represent the shape of the picture. 'S' means a circle, 'P' means a triangle, 'T' means a square and 'Q' means a T-shape.

Step 5:

Now that you know what the second letter means, go to the answer picture and eliminate the remaining wrong answer. The answer picture is a square, so that would make the last letter a 'T'.

From earlier you were left with answers 'A' and 'D'. Now you can fill in the second letter and get your answer. The answer letters are 'ET' so the answer is 'A'.

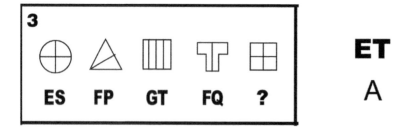

Q4)

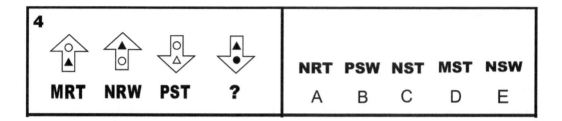

					NRT	PSW	NST	MST	NSW
MRT	NRW	PST	?		A	B	C	D	E

Step 1:

Cover the pictures and find the recurring letters. You should have found the letters 'R' and 'T'.

Step 2:

It doesn't matter which recurring set of letters you choose to work out first. (I am going to pick 'T' to work out first.) So look at the pictures represented by the letter 'T' and find what is the same in them.

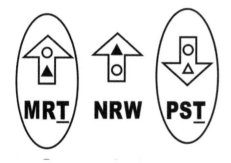

You should have found three things:
1) They are both arrows.
2) They both contain a triangle and circle.
3) The both have the circle above the triangle.

So now you look at the other picture and check to see what one it is. The other picture is also an arrow and also contains a circle and triangle, so it is not numbers 1 or 2. This means that 'T' represents a circle above the triangle in the picture. You now also know that 'W' means a triangle above the circle.

Step 3:
Using what you found in Step 2, go to the answer picture and work out the last letter. In the answer picture the triangle is above the circle, so the last letter would be a 'W'. This eliminates answers 'A', 'C' and 'D'.

Step 4:
Now take another set of recurring letters. As there is only one, look at the pictures that are represented by the letter 'R' and find what is the same in them.

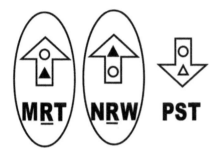

You should see that both are arrows facing in the same direction. (You will note that they are both arrows, but as we have already established that all three pictures contain arrows, it cannot be that alone.) You now know that 'R' means the arrow is pointing up and 'S' means the arrow is pointing down.

Step 5:
Now that you know what the middle letter represents, go to the answer picture and eliminate more answers. The answer picture is an arrow pointing down, so the middle letter will be 'S'.

From earlier you were left with answers 'B' and 'E', now you can potentially eliminate another answer. The letters you have so far are '?SW', but this does not help you filter another answer, so you must find out what the first letter means.

Step 6:
As all of the recurring letters are gone, this shows that the first letter means that the pictures are all different in the same way.

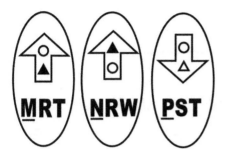

So look at all of the pictures, you should see that for the picture represented by an 'M' the bottom inside shape is shaded, for the 'N' picture the top shape is shaded and for the 'P' picture both of the inside shapes are the same, un-shaded.

Step 7:

Now you know what the first letter represents you can eliminate the remaining wrong answer. The answer picture has both inside shapes shaded, so the first letter will be an 'M'. (They are both the same, although in the question picture represented by the letter 'P' the shapes are un-shaded, they are both THE SAME.)

From earlier you were left with answers 'B' and 'E'. You can now fill in the first letter and get your answer. The answer letters are 'PSW' so the answer is 'B'.

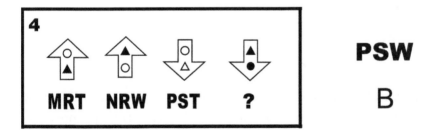

PSW

B

Q5)

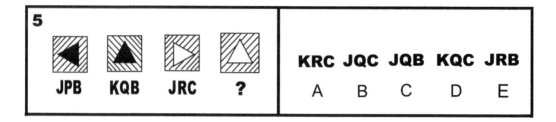

Step 1:
Cover the pictures and find the recurring letters. You should have found the letters 'J' and 'B'.

Step 2:
It doesn't matter which recurring set of letters you choose to work out first. (I am going to pick 'J' to work out first.) So look at the pictures represented by the letter 'J' and find what is the same in them.

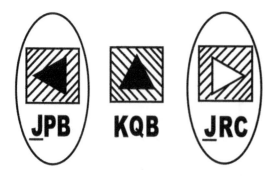

You should have found that both of those pictures are shaded in the same way, diagonally in a bottom-left to top-right fashion. Now you know that 'K' represents the picture being shaded diagonally in the opposite direction, top-left to bottom-right.

Step 3:
Now that you know what the first letter represents, go to the answer picture and filter out the wrong answers. The answer picture is shaded diagonally bottom-left to top-right so the first letter will be a 'J'. This eliminates answers 'A' and 'D'.

Step 4:

Now take the remaining set of recurring letters, 'B', and find out what is the same in the pictures represented by that letter.

You should see that both of those pictures have a shaded triangle in the center, now you know that the letter 'B' represents a shaded triangle and the letter 'C' represents an un-shaded triangle.

Step 5:

Now you know what the last letter represents, go to the answer picture and eliminate more answers. The answer picture has an un-shaded triangle, so the last letter will be 'C'.

From earlier you were left with answers 'B', 'C' and 'E', now you can potentially eliminate more answers. The letters you have so far are 'J?C', and this leaves you with only one answer, 'B'.

Step 6:

So the answer is 'B', but as you haven't figured out what the middle letter represents, you can work it out to check that your answer is correct.

So look at all of the pictures, as none of the middle letters match, and find what is different in the same way.

You should see that all of the pictures contain a triangle facing in different directions. So the middle letter must represent the direction the triangle is facing: 'P' means left, 'Q' means up and 'R' means right.

Step 7:
As you already have your answer ('B'), see if the middle letter matches what you just found. The arrow is pointing up, so the middle letter should be 'Q'. The answer 'B' is 'JQC' so now you know for sure that you are correct.

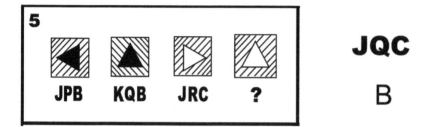

JQC

B

YOUR OWN ADDITIONAL NOTES

Use this page to write down important points you have picked up from this topic, and any additional information you would like to add:

ODD ONE OUT

Unfortunately there are no steps for finding the Odd One Out, however there are a lot of things to look out for when working out the questions:

THINGS TO LOOK FOR

- Shaded/un-shaded
- Direction (must find base point first)
- Size of picture
- Number of sides of each picture (odd, even, equal etc.)
- Outline of picture (dotted, solid, thick, thin)
- Inside the picture (patterns, other shapes/symbols)
- Amount of shapes/symbols in the picture
- Curved or straight lines (how many?)
- Overlapping or under-lapping shapes/symbols
- Regular or irregular shapes
- Order that shapes/lines appear in

HINT

If you can, you must make sure that before you look at every picture in the question, you find the BASE POINT. This is a must-do in order to avoid confusion and getting the wrong answer. (Use this technique when all the pictures appear the same but are in different positions.)

Odd One Out Questions

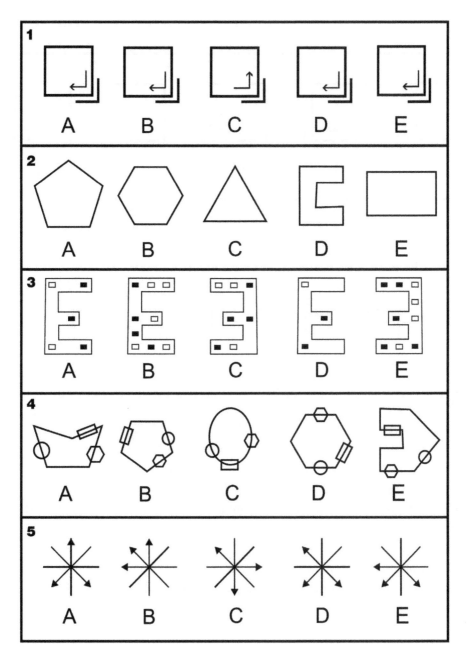

First try to answer these using the notes

1) ____   2) ____   3) ____   4) ____   5) ____

Working out ODD ONE OUT

Q1)

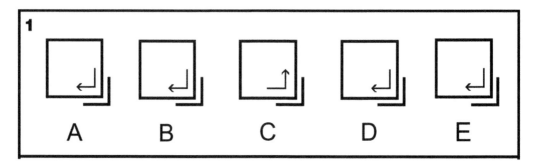

With this question, all pictures are the same shape and all have an arrow in a corner so it is a perfect question to use the 'Finding a Base Point' method.

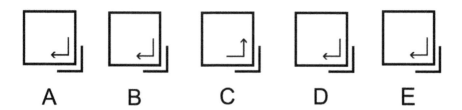

First, set where you want your base point – I'll pick having the arrow in the bottom-right corner. So now you must look at every picture with the arrow in the bottom-right corner. (Turn the paper so that when you look at each picture the arrow is in the bottom-right corner, there are no rules against turning your paper in any direction to help work out an answer.)

Now you should see that answer picture 'C' is the odd one out because the arrow is facing in the opposite direction to the rest, so 'C' is the answer.

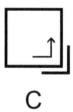

Q2)

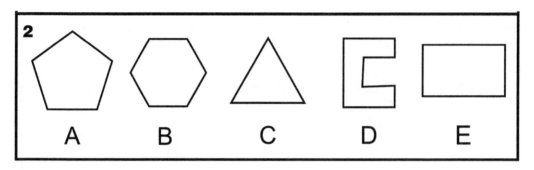

For this question, two things should come to mind when you look at it. First – how many sides does each picture shape have? Second – are the picture shapes regular or not?

After counting the sides of the shape, they are all different, and some are odd and some are even, so the answer isn't based on this. Next, look at the types of shape, they are all regular shapes, except for one. So the answer will be 'D' as it is the only irregular shape.

D

Q3)

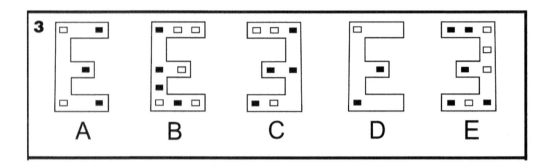

For this question, finding a base point is useless as the position of the squares in each picture is different. Looking at the question, you should think to first count the number of squares in each picture to see if only one has an odd or even amount. This is not the case, so next check how many shaded and un-shaded squares there are in each picture.

You should have found that in all of the pictures except one there is exactly one more shaded square than the number of un-shaded squares in that picture. Only answer 'B' has the opposite rule, that picture contains more un-shaded squares than shaded squares. So 'B' is the answer.

B

Q4)

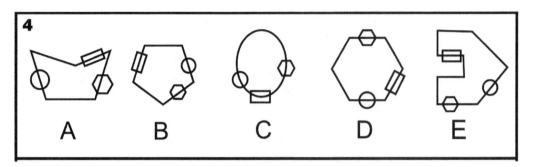

At first glance there may seem to be no odd one out. The pictures are a mixture of regular and irregular shapes, so that doesn't help you. Next, all of the pictures contain the same three smaller shapes: a circle, rectangle and a hexagon.

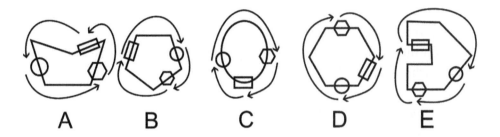

Now it is time to look at the order that the smaller shapes appear in. You should find that there is only one picture where the order of the shapes is not a circle, then a hexagon then a rectangle in a clockwise fashion around the large shape.

A

So the answer is 'A' as the order of the smaller shapes around the bigger shape in a clockwise fashion is a circle, a rectangle and then a hexagon.

A

Q5)

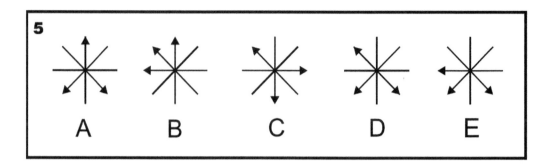

This question requires you to look at each picture carefully. The first thought should be to count the number of arrow tips each picture has, but as they all have three this doesn't help you.

Next look at the placement of each arrow tip in relation to the others in that picture. Upon doing so you should notice that there is only one picture that has two arrow tips directly opposite each other.

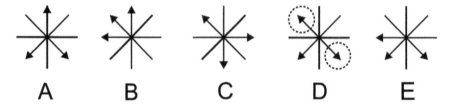

So you know that the answer is 'D'.

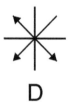

D

YOUR OWN ADDITIONAL NOTES

Use this page to write down important points you have picked up from this topic, and any additional information you would like to add:

SEQUENCES

Step 1:
Find where to start.

- If the answer box is in the first two boxes, then you start from the right.
- If the answer box is in the last two boxes, then you start from the left.
- If the answer box is in the middle then you can start from either side.

This is done to give you the best chance of working out the question, as you will have more information available to you when working out the next steps.

Step 2:
Break down the pictures in the boxes before the answer box. (Remember that if you are starting from the right then you work your way backwards.) E.g. – how many shapes/symbols are there? Are they overlapping or under-lapping shapes? What is shaded, what is un-shaded? Etc.

Step 3:
Now take one of the things that you have broken down from Step 2 and look at how it changes from box to box.

HINT

If the answer box is not the first or last box, then as you are viewing the change from box to box, try and think where what you are looking for would be, and see if that fits the pattern as you continue along the sequence. (Also see 'THINGS TO LOOK FOR'.)

Step 4:
Use what you found from Step 3 to eliminate incorrect answers. (You should have found

where the position of whatever you are looking for would be within the answer box, so eliminate all answer boxes accordingly.)

★★You can now eliminate incorrect answers★★

Step 5:
Go back to Step 3 and repeat the process until you have found the correct answer.

THINGS TO LOOK FOR
(This will help with Step 3)

- Rotation/direction
- Size change
- Overlapping/under-lapping
- Shaded/unshaded
- More shapes/symbols or less shapes/symbols
- Does anything alternate? (Do the shapes/symbols keep switching with each other? Does it go from shaded to unshaded then back to shaded and keep repeating? Do the lines go from solid to dotted then back and keep repeating? Etc.)
- Number of sides
- Replacement

Sequences Questions

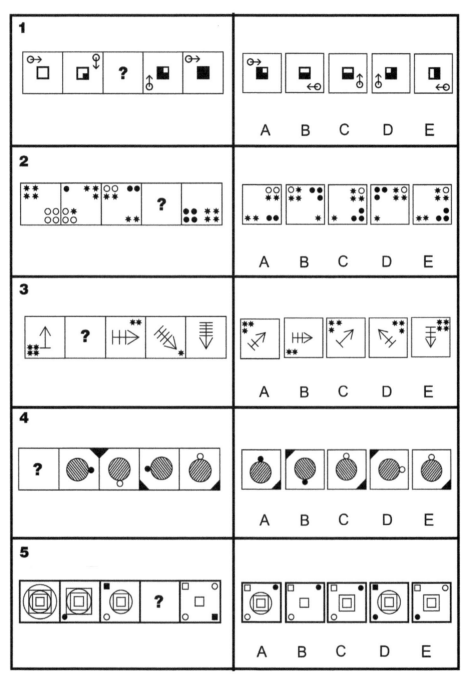

First try to answer these using the notes

1) _____   2) _____   3) _____   4) _____   5) _____

Working out SEQUENCES

Q1)

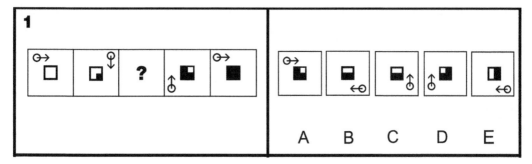

Step 1:
As the answer box is the third box in the sequence, in the middle, it doesn't matter which end you start at. (I will pick the left side to start, so every time I look at the sequence it will be from left to right.)

Step 2:
When breaking down the pictures in the boxes before the answer box, you should have found the following:
a)   A circle with an arrow
b)   A square in the center of each box

Step 3:
Take one of the things you found and look at how it changes from box to box. (I'll take 'a'.)

a) A circle with an arrow – you should see that the circle with the arrow moves to the corner the arrow is facing, as you go from box to box. This also means that the arrow is facing the corner that the circle will move to in the next box.

Step 4:
Use what you have just found from Step 3 to eliminate wrong answers. You know that the circle with the arrow should be in the bottom-right corner of the answer box as that is where the arrow from box two in the sequence is pointing. You also know that the arrow in the answer box should be pointing towards the bottom-left corner as that is where the circle in box four of the sequence is. You should have eliminated answers 'A', 'C' and 'D'.

Step 5:
Now go back and take another thing you found in Step 2 and view the change from box to box. You must take 'b'.

b) A square in the center of each box – you should see that from box to box a quarter of shading is added to the square. You should also see that the shading gets added in a clockwise fashion.

Step 6:
Now go to the answer pictures and use what you have found to filter out more wrong answers. You were left with answers 'B' and 'E' from before, you should have now eliminated 'E' as the shaded quarter gets added in an anticlockwise fashion, not clockwise as you wanted. So the answer is 'B'.

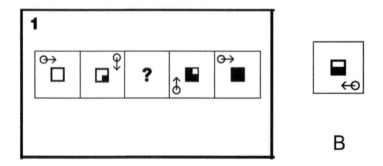

B

Q2)

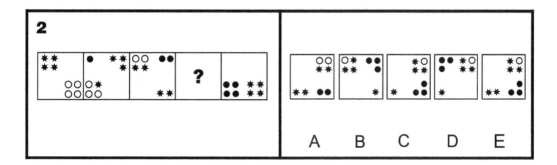

Step 1:
As the answer box is the fourth box in the sequence, you must start at the left of the sequence.

Step 2:
When breaking down the pictures in the boxes before the answer box, you should have found the following:
a) Shaded stars
b) Unshaded circles
c) Shaded circles

Step 3:
Take one of the things you found and look at how it changes from box to box. (I'll take 'a'.)

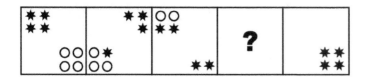

a) Shaded stars – you should see that the shaded stars move from corner to corner in a clockwise fashion as you go from box to box. You should also see that one of the shaded stars replaces an un-shaded circle as this happens (it moves to the opposite corner and takes the place of an un-shaded circle).

Step 4:

Use what you have just found to eliminate wrong answers. Start with the main group of shaded stars, you should see that in the answer picture, there should be one shaded star in the bottom-left corner of the box. This also means that there will be three shaded stars in the corner opposite. You should have eliminated answers 'A', 'B' and 'E'.

Step 5:

Now go back and take another thing you found in Step 2 and view the change from box to box. (I'll take 'b'.)

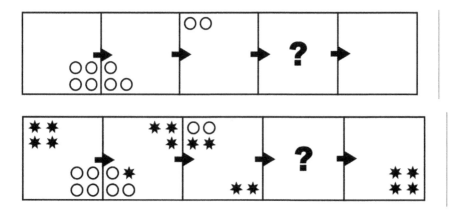

b) Unshaded circles – you should see that the un-shaded circles move from corner to corner in a clockwise fashion as you go from box to box. You should also see that there is always one less un-shaded circle as you go from box to box, the un-shaded circle gets replaced with a star.

REMEMBER – you are only looking at the unshaded circles at the moment, so forget about the shaded ones for now.

Step 6:

Now go to the answer pictures and use what you have found to filter out more wrong answers. You were left with answers 'C' and 'D' from before, you should now still have answers 'C' and 'D', as they both have one unshaded circle with three stars in the corner that you want them to be in. This step didn't help in filtering out any answers this time, but it did help you check to see that out of the answers you have left, one of them is definitely correct.

Step 7:

Now go back and take another thing you found in Step 2 and view the change from box to box. You must take 'c'.

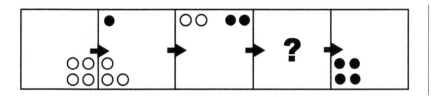

c) Shaded circles – you should see that the shaded circles also move from corner to corner in a clockwise fashion as you go from box to box. You should also see that the number of shaded circles increases by one as you go from box to box.

Step 8:

Now go to the answer pictures and use what you have found to filter the remaining wrong answer. You were left with answers 'C' and 'D' from before, you should have now eliminated answer 'D' as although there are three shaded circles, they are not in the corner you want them in. So the answer is 'C'.

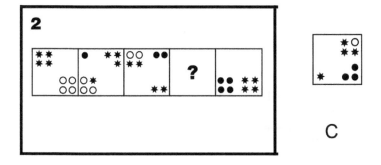

C

Q3)

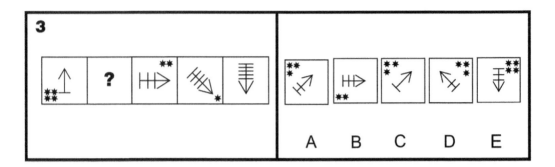

Step 1:
As the answer box is the second box in the sequence, you must start at the right of the sequence (and work backwards).

Step 2:
When breaking down the pictures in the boxes before the answer box, you should have found the following:
a) An arrow with lines
b) Stars

Step 3:
Take one of the things you found and look at how it changes from box to box. (I'll take 'b'.) REMEMBER – you are looking from right to left when viewing the changes.

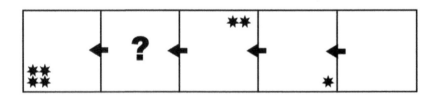

b) Stars – you should see that the stars move in a clockwise fashion around the picture as you move from box to box. You should also see that there is a star added as you move from box to box.

Step 4:
Use what you have just found from Step 3 to eliminate wrong answers. You know that the stars should be in the top-left corner of the box, and there should be three of them. You should have eliminated answers 'B', 'D' and 'E'.

Step 5:
Now go back and take another thing you found in Step 2 and view the change from box to box. You must take 'a'.

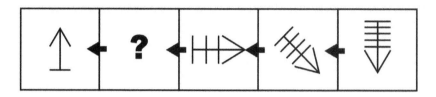

a) An arrow with lines – you should see that the arrow rotates anticlockwise 45° as you go from box to box. You should also see that the lines on the arrow decrease by one as you move from box to box.

Step 6:
Now go to the answer pictures and use what you have found to filter out more wrong answers. You were left with answers 'A' and 'C' from before, you should now have eliminated 'C' as although it is facing in the correct direction, there should be two lines on the arrow. So the answer is 'A'.

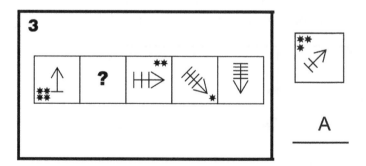

A
___

Q4)

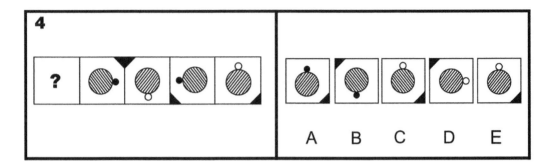

Step 1:
As the answer box is the first box in the sequence, you must start at the right of the sequence (and work backwards).

Step 2:
When breaking down the pictures in the boxes before the answer box, you should have found the following:
a)   A large circle
b)   A small circle
c)   A triangle

Step 3:
Take one of the things you found and look at how it changes from box to box. (I'll take 'c'.) REMEMBER – you are looking from right to left when viewing the changes.

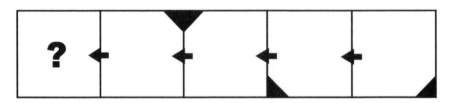

c) A triangle – you should see that the triangle remains shaded and moves from corner to corner in a clockwise fashion as you go from box to box.

Step 4:

Use what you have just found from Step 3 to eliminate wrong answers. You know that in the answer picture the shaded triangle should be in the bottom-right corner of the box. You should have eliminated answers 'A', 'B' and 'D'.

Step 5:

Now go back and take another thing you found in Step 2 and view the change from box to box. (I'll take 'a'.)

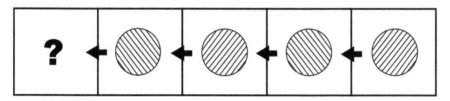

a) A large circle – you should see that whilst the large circle remains in the same position, the diagonal shading alternates (switches from one to the other then back) as you go from box to box.

Step 6:

Now go to the answer pictures and use what you have found to filter out more wrong answers. You were left with answers 'C' and 'E' from before, you should now have eliminated answer 'C' as the diagonal shading is not in the correct direction.

So the answer is 'E'.

Step 7:

Although you already have your answer, as you have one more thing that you found in Step 1 left, you can use this to check your answer to make sure it is correct. So go back and take the last thing you found in Step 2: this is 'b'.

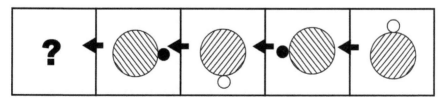

b) A small circle – you should see that the small circle rotates 90° anticlockwise around the large circle. You should also see that the small circle alternates between shaded and un-shaded as you go from box to box.

Step 8:
As you already have your answer, you are using what you have found to check it. You know that the small circle should be at the top of the large circle, and it should also be unshaded. This is the case in answer 'E', so you know that you have the correct answer.

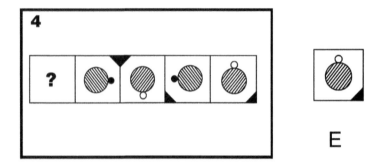

E

Q5)

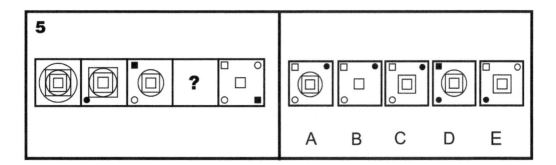

Step 1:
As the answer box is the fourth box in the sequence, you must start at the left of the sequence.

Step 2:
When breaking down the pictures in the boxes before the answer box, you should have found the following:
a) Center square
b) Squares
c) Circles

There are also two more things to note, which bring all of the above things that you found together.
d) The shapes are inside each other
e) The number of shapes in the corner of the box and their shade (are they shaded or not)

Step 3:
Take one of the things you found that brings all of the others together ('d' or 'e') and look at how it changes from box to box. This is because you will be using the other things that you found whilst viewing these changes. (I'll take 'd'.)

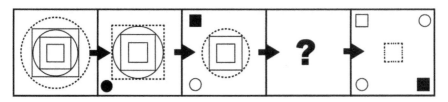

d) The shapes are inside each other – you should see that as you move from box to box the shape that was on the outside of the center shapes in the previous box, moves to a corner and becomes shaded. You should also see that the remaining shapes in the center stay in the same place.

Step 4:
Use what you have just found to eliminate wrong answers. You know that there should be a shaded circle in the corner of the answer box as a circle was the outside center shape in the picture box before. You also know that the outside center shape will be a square and the order of the remaining center shapes will stay the same from the previous box. You should have eliminated answers 'A', 'B' and 'D'. Although they all have a shaded circle in a corner, the shapes in the center are not how you want them.

Step 5:
Now go back and take another thing you found in Step 2 and view the change from box to box. You must take 'e'.

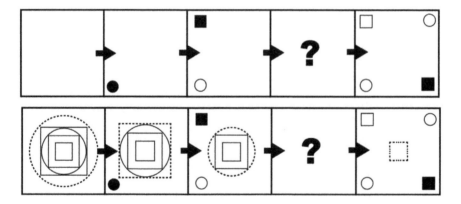

e) The number of shapes in the corner of the box and their shade – you should see that the number of shapes in the corner of each picture increases by one as you go from box to box. You should also see that the new shape in the corner of the box is shaded, and was the outside center shape of the box before. There is also never more than one shaded shape in a box.

Step 6:

Now go to the answer pictures and use what you have found to filter out more wrong answers. You were left with answers 'C' and 'E' from before, you should have now eliminated answer 'E' because although the amount of shapes are correct, the wrong circle is shaded, the new circle that appears is supposed to be shaded.
So the answer is 'C'.

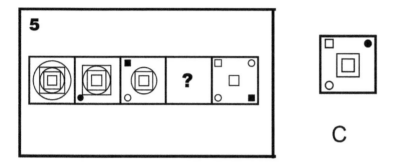

C

YOUR OWN ADDITIONAL NOTES

Use this page to write down important points you have picked up from this topic, and any additional information you would like to add:

MOST IN COMMON

We ONLY find the things that are in common (the same) between the question pictures, then use that to help us find our answer. Remember that this is MOST IN COMMON, not 'exactly the same', so just find the one (or two) answers that have more in common than the other answers

As with Odd One Out there are no steps for finding the Most in Common, however there are a lot of things to look out for when working out the questions:

> HINT
> If you cant find anything in common at first glance,
> then look at the separate question pictures
> individually and break them down (focus on one
> thing within that picture).

THINGS TO LOOK FOR

- Shaded/unshaded
- Objects inside the shape (how many?)
- Patterns inside the shapes/symbols
- Outline (solid, dotted, thick, thin)
- Total number of sides in each question picture
- Symmetry
- Size
- Number of shapes/symbols in total in each question picture
- Regular/irregular shapes
- Parallel/perpendicular lines (how many?)
- Overlapping/under-lapping shapes
- Curved/straight lines (how many)
- Are the shapes/symbols the same in each question picture?

Most in Common Questions

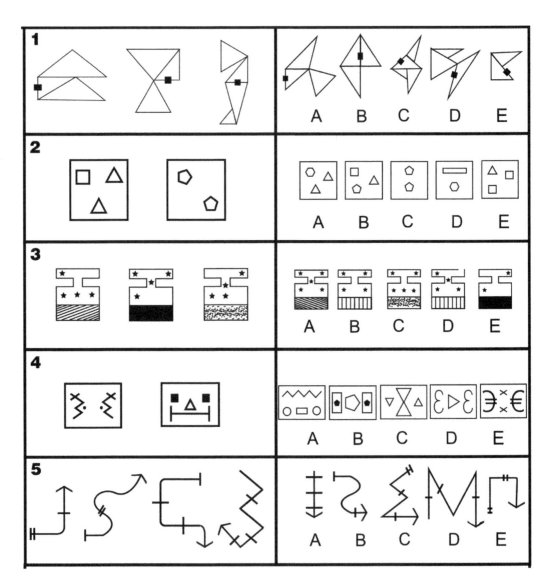

First try to answer these using the notes

1) ____   2) ____   3) ____   4) ____   5) ____

Working out MOST IN COMMON

Q1)

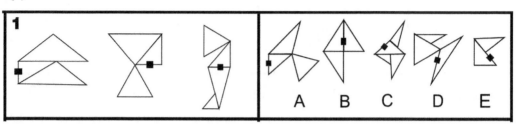

Look at the question pictures. Find all the things that are in common. You should have found the following:

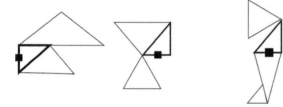

1) All pictures contain a shaded square
2) The shaded square is always on the short side of the right-angled triangle in all of the pictures.

Now that you have found all of the things in common, go to the answer pictures and filter out the wrong answers until you are left with the correct one.

1) All pictures contain a shaded square – all of the answer pictures contain a shaded square so this doesn't help you at all.
2) The shaded square is always on the short side of the right-angled triangle in all of the pictures – there is only one picture where the shaded square is on the short side of the right-angled triangle, so the answer is 'A'.

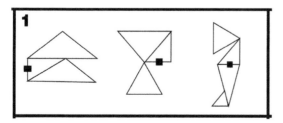

Q2)

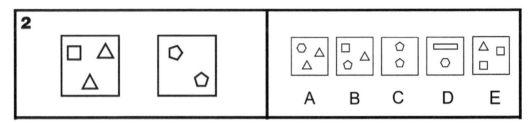

Look at the question pictures. Find all the things that are in common. You should have found the following:

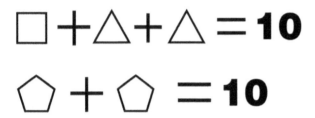

1) In both of the pictures, the number of sides of the shapes totals ten when added together.

Now that you have found all of the things in common, go to the answer pictures and filter out the wrong answers until you are left with the correct one.

1) In both of the pictures, the number of sides of the shapes totals ten when added together – after counting all of the sides in each answer picture, you should find your answer which is 'D'.

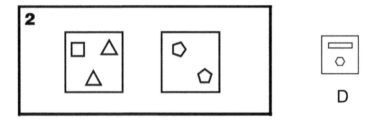

Q3)

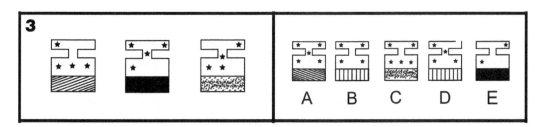

Look at the question pictures. Find all the things that are in common. You should have found the following:

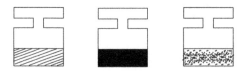

1) The smaller part of each picture shape is half shaded.

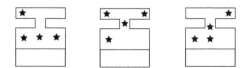

2) There are four stars in each picture.

3) All of the pictures are the same complete shape.

Now that you have found all of the things in common, go to the answer pictures and filter out the wrong answers until you are left with the correct one.

1) The smaller part of each picture shape is half shaded – all of the answer pictures have the smaller part of the shape shaded so this doesn't help you at all.

2) There are four stars in each picture – after going through all of the answer pictures you should be left with two possible answers, 'B' and 'D' as they both contain four stars.

3) All of the pictures are the same complete shape – you only need to look at answer pictures 'B' and 'D' as these are the two answers left. You should see that 'D' is an incomplete shape, so the answer is 'B'.

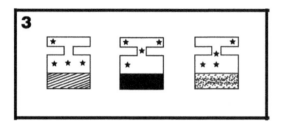

B

Q4)

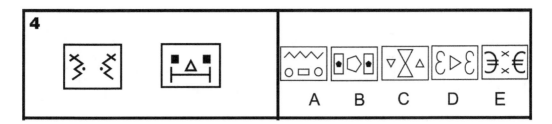

Look at the question pictures. Find all the things that are in common. You should have found the following:

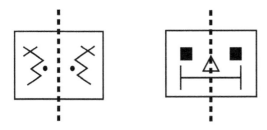

1) The pictures are both symmetrical through a vertical line in the center of the picture.

Now that you have found all of the things in common, go to the answer pictures and filter out the wrong answers until you are left with the correct one.

2) The pictures are both symmetrical through a vertical line in the center of the picture – there is only one answer picture that is symmetrical like that, so the answer is 'E'.

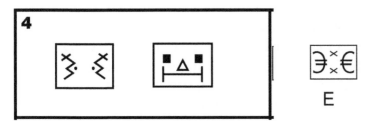

NOTE:

- Answer picture 'A' looks symmetrical in the same way at first glance, however the zigzag line is not symmetrical in any way.
- Answer picture 'B' has a line of symmetry however the line is horizontal, don't confuse this with the vertical line of symmetry.

Q5)

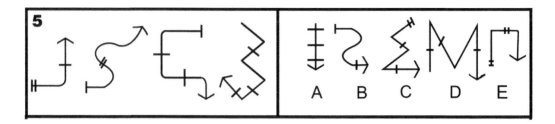

Look at the question pictures. Find all the things that are in common. You should have found the following:

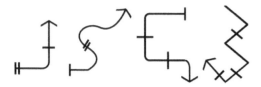

1) All of the pictures have three lines on the arrow.

2) None of the pictures have a totally straight arrow, they all bend in some form.

Now that you have found all of the things in common, go to the answer pictures and filter out the wrong answers until you are left with the correct one.

1) All of the pictures have three lines on the arrow – after looking through the answer pictures you should be left with answers 'A' and 'D'.
2) None of the pictures have a totally straight arrow, they all bend in some form – remember this is Most In Common, so although it may seem like there are two answers as 'A' is a totally straight arrow, the answer must be 'D' as that answer picture has the MOST in common with the question pictures.

So the answer is 'D'.

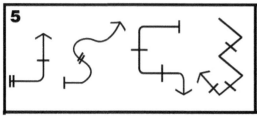

YOUR OWN ADDITIONAL NOTES

Use this page to write down important points you have picked up from this topic, and any additional information you would like to add:

MATRICES

Matrices are solved using either the Analogies method, Sequences method or seeing a visual pattern

Step 1:

Find out what method you will be using. If it is a four-squared matrix use the Analogies method, if it is a nine-squared matrix use the Sequences method. You may also solve the question in one step using the Visual Pattern method for either a four or nine-squared matrix, however this method is normally only used to try and solve nine-squared matrices.

> HINT
> Always try the Visual Pattern method first.

Visual Pattern Method

Step 2:

This is simply looking for a visual pattern in the matrix as a whole picture, rather than looking at the individual squares. Then find the answer box that would complete the pattern. This would normally involve symmetry but not always.

> HINT
> Very few questions can be solved using this method, so if you cannot see the pattern within the first five to six seconds, move on to using either the Analogies or Sequences method.

WORKING OUT A FOUR-SQUARED MATRIX

Using the Analogies method to solve the question:

Step 3:
Find the question analogy. You do this by finding the row or column of boxes that look similar. The other row/column will contain the box that we have to find the answer to.

Step 4:
Work out the rest of the question starting from Step 1 using the Analogies method:

Step A:
Break down the first picture they give you (the question analogy).

Step B:
Take one thing out of the broken down picture and view the transformation (see how it changes).

```
                            HINT
             Remember your 'THINGS TO LOOK FOR'
```

Step C:
Now go to the answer picture and emulate what you did from Step 2. (Copy the change from Step B using the appropriate shape in the answer picture.)

You can now eliminate incorrect answers

Step D:
Go back to Step B and repeat as necessary.

WORKING OUT A NINE-SQUARED MATRIX

Using the Sequences method:

Step 3:
Find where to start.

If the answer box is in the first four squares, start at the bottom-right square and work up, going backwards along the rows.

If the answer box is in the last four squares, start at the top-left square and work down going forwards along the rows.

If the answer box is in the middle square, first check that you have not missed a visual pattern. If you haven't, then start from either the top-left or bottom-right square.

Step 4:
Work out the rest of the question starting from Step 2 using the Sequences method:

Step A:
Break down the pictures in the boxes before the answer box. (Remember that if you are starting from the right then you work your way backwards.)

Step B:
Now take one of the things that you have broken down from Step A and look at how it changes from box to box.

Step C:
Use what you found from Step B to eliminate incorrect answers. (You should have found where what you are looking for would be within the answer box, so eliminate all answer boxes accordingly.)

★★You can now eliminate incorrect answers★★

Step D:
Go back to Step B and repeat the process until you have found the correct answer.

THINGS TO LOOK FOR

(This will help with ALL methods)

- Shaded/unshaded
- Alternating shapes/symbols
- Lines (straight, curved, dashed, thin etc.)
- Position inside the box
- Direction/rotation
- Size
- Horizontal/vertical/diagonal shading or lines

HINT
Remember to go to the correct section (Analogies or Sequences) for further 'THINGS TO LOOK FOR' and 'HINTS' for the specified type of matrix you are going to solve.

Matrices Questions

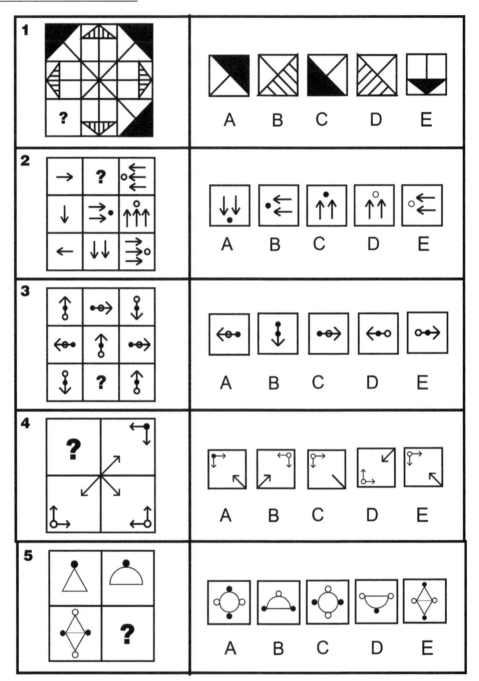

First try to answer these using the notes

1) ____   2) ____   3) ____   4) ____   5) ____

Working out MATRICES

Q1)

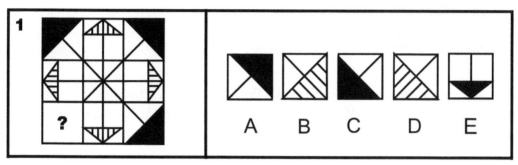

Step 1:
It is a nine-squared matrix, so you will be using the Sequences method if the Visual Pattern method doesn't work.

Step 2:
First try the Visual Pattern method – glance over the matrix as a whole (as if it is one big square, not nine little ones) and see if it forms an image or picture. REMEMBER – this technique usually involves looking for symmetry.

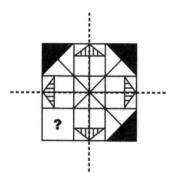

You should see that there are two lines of symmetry that are clearly visible, horizontal and vertical lines running through the middle of the picture. So you can use this method to complete the question.

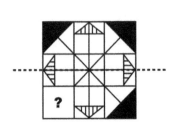

Now take one of the lines of symmetry and find the answer. I'll take the horizontal line, so look at the completed half of the picture (the top half) and in your head, reflect it to the bottom. You should see that the answer box you want should contain an arrow pointing to the bottom-left of the box, and it should have solid shading.

You have now found your answer box, which is answer 'C'.

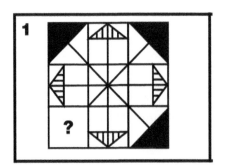

C

Q2)

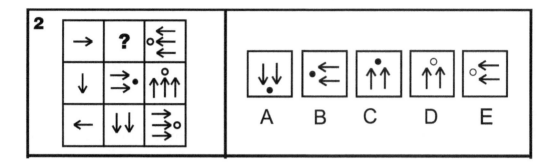

Step 1:

It is a nine-squared matrix, so you will be using the Sequences method if the Visual Pattern method doesn't work.

Step 2:

First try the Visual Pattern method – glance over the matrix as a whole (as if it is one big square, not nine little ones) and see if it forms an image or picture.

You should see that is doesn't, so move on to the Sequences method quickly.

Step 3:

As the answer box is in the second box in the sequence, you will start in the bottom-left box of the matrix (and work backwards, right to left, bottom to top).

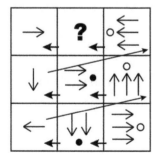

Step 4:

Now use the Sequences technique you have learnt to work out the rest of the question.

Step 4a:

When breaking down the pictures in the boxes before the answer box, you should have found the following:

a) Arrows

b) Circles

Step 4b:

Take one of the things you found and look at how it changes from box to box. (I'll take 'b'.)

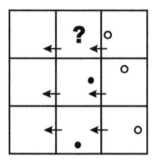

b) Circles – you should see that the order goes: un-shaded circle, shaded circle then no circle, and then that sequence repeats.

Step 4c:

Use what you have just found to eliminate wrong answers. You should know that there should be a shaded circle in the answer box. You should have eliminated answers 'D' and 'E'.

Step 4d:

Now go back and take another thing you found in Step 4a and view the change from box to box. You must take 'a'.

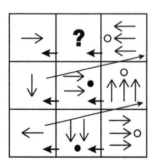

a) Arrows – you should see that the number of arrows goes from three to two to one as you go from box to box, and then repeats. You should also see that the arrow rotates 90° clockwise as you go from box to box.

Step 4e:

Now go to the answer pictures and use what you have found to filter out more wrong answers. You were left with answers 'A', 'B' and 'C' from before, you should now have eliminated answers 'A' and 'B' as the arrows in those pictures are facing the wrong direction. So the answer is 'C'.

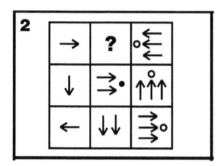

C

Q3)

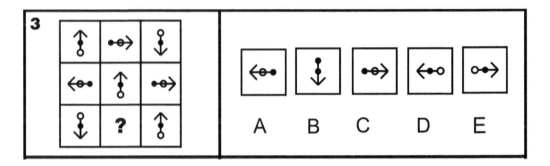

Step 1:
It is a nine-squared matrix, so you will be using the Sequences method if the Visual Pattern method doesn't work.

Step 2:
First try the Visual Pattern method – glance over the matrix as a whole (as if it is one big square, not nine little ones) and see if it forms an image or picture.
You should see that is doesn't, so move on to the Sequences method quickly.

Step 3:
As the answer box is the eighth box in the sequence (looking at the matrix from left to right, top down), you will start in the top-left box of the matrix.

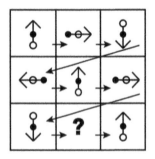

Step 4:
Now use the Sequences technique you have learnt to work out the rest of the question.

Step 4a:

When breaking down the pictures in the boxes before the answer box, you should have found the following:

a) An arrow

b) Two circles, one at the end of the arrow and one in the center.

Step 4b:

Take one of the things you found and look at how it changes from box to box. (I'll take 'a'.)

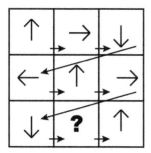

a) An arrow – you should see that the arrow rotates 90° clockwise as you move from box to box.

Step 4c:

Use what you have just found to eliminate wrong answers. You should know that the arrow in the answer box will be facing to the left. You should have eliminated answers 'B', 'C' and 'E'.

Step 4d:

Now go back and take another thing you found in Step 4a and view the change from box to box. You must take 'b'.

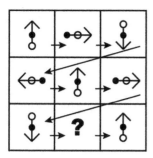

b) Two circles, one at the end of the arrow and one in the center – you should see that the circle on the end of the arrow swaps with the circle in the center of the arrow every time you move from box to box.

Step 4e:

Now go to the answer pictures and use what you have found to filter out more wrong answers. You were left with answers 'A' and 'D' from before, you should have now eliminated answer 'D' as the circle at the end of the arrow should be shaded, and the other circle un-shaded. So your answer is 'A'.

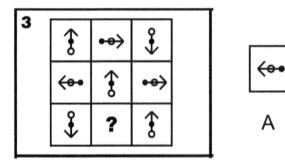

Q4)

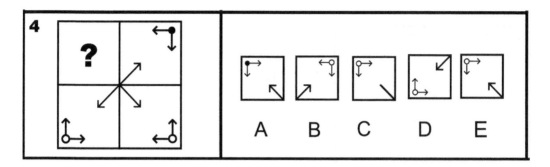

A   B   C   D   E

Step 1:
It is a four-squared matrix, so you will be using the Analogies method if the Visual Pattern method doesn't work.

Step 2:
First try the Visual Pattern method – glance over the matrix as a whole (as if it is one big square, not four small ones) and see if it forms an image or picture.

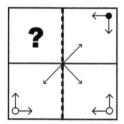

You should see that there is one line of symmetry, a vertical line running through the center of the picture. So you can use this method to complete the question.

Now take the vertical line and look at the completed half of the picture (the right half) and in your head, reflect it to the left side. You should see that the answer picture you want will contain a shaded circle in the top-left corner of the box, and the arrows coming out of it will point to the right and down. You should also see that there should be an arrow from the bottom-right of the box coming out half way and pointing to the top-left of the box.

You have now found your answer box, which is answer 'A'.

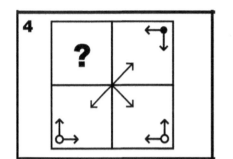

A

Q5)

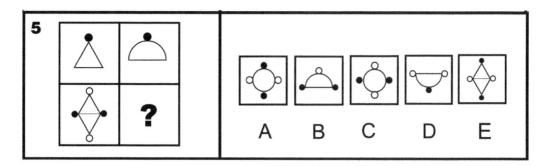

Step 1:
It is a four-squared matrix, so you will be using the Analogies method if the Visual Pattern method doesn't work.

Step 2:
First try the Visual Pattern method – glance over the matrix as a whole (as if it is one big square, not four small ones) and see if it forms an image or picture. You should see that is doesn't, so move on to the Analogies method quickly.

Step 3:
You should have found that the question analogy will be the top-left box to the bottom-left box (the left column) as they look similar, and the answer analogy will be the top-right box to the bottom-right box (the right column). As the answer box is at the bottom of the answer analogy, you will look at the question analogy from top to bottom.

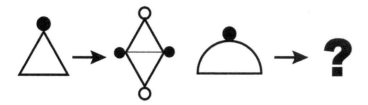

Step 4:
Now use the Analogies technique you have learnt to work out the rest of the question.

Step 4a:

Break down the first picture in the question analogy (the top-left box). You should have found the following:
a) A triangle
b) A shaded circle

Step 4b:
Take one of the things you found and view the transformation. (I'll take 'a'.)

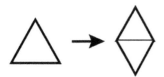

a) A triangle – you should see that the triangle has another triangle that has been rotated 180° and placed under it to form a diamond. You should also see that the bottom line of the triangle disappears.

Step 4c:
Now go to the answer question and use what you have just found to filter out wrong answers. You know that the answer box should have a circle in the middle with no line across it. (The circle is created by rotating another semi-circle at 180° and adding it under the existing semi-circle and then removing the line.) You should now have eliminated answers 'B', 'D' and 'E'.

Step 4d:
Now go back and take another thing you found in Step 4a and view the transformation. You must take 'b'.

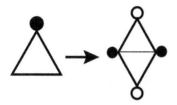

b) A shaded circle – you should see that the shaded circle becomes un-shaded. You should also see that three more circles appear, to form four circles opposite each other on the sides of the center shape. You should also see that the circles opposite each other are matching in shade.

Step 4e:

Now go to the answer question and use what you have found to filter out more wrong answers. You were left with answers 'A' and 'C' from before, you should have now eliminated answer 'A' as although there are four circles and the opposite circles match in shade, the top circle should be un-shaded. That would make the top and bottom circles un-shaded, and the side circle shaded. So the answer is 'C'.

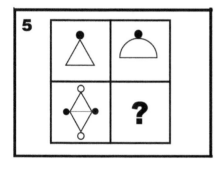

C

YOUR OWN ADDITIONAL NOTES

Use this page to write down important points you have picked up from this topic, and any additional information you would like to add: